# the table

I0617554

POWER HOUSE

# the table

*Your seat is waiting for you.*

Jason Houston

Cover and interior book design by Michelle Everett for POWER HOUSE, © 2023 Power House Studios, LLC.

Published by: **Power House**

An imprint of Power House Studios LLC.

thepowerhousestudio.com

PO Box 101678

Cape Coral FL 33910

Home of *The Power House Blueprint*™ Concierge Publishing System

# Dedication

This book is lovingly dedicated to our precious faithful WORD4Life Partners! Thank you for your continuous prayers and financial support. You have made this dream a reality.

I love and appreciate you all! There is Life in the WORD for you!

# Acknowledgments

Our Lord! What a tremendous experience it has been to write this book. I am eternally grateful for the leading, guiding, and teaching of the Holy Spirit. I give thanks and praise to God the Father for the precious gift of His Son, Jesus! He has been so real and so precious during this time. May this book bring glory and honor to His Name.

Evangelist Linda Brewer is ready and willing to minister anywhere at any time. The Holy Ghost uses this mighty woman of God in a spectacularly powerful and precious way.

Evangelist Nancy Harmon, the one and only true Queen of Gospel Music. Her ministry has shaped and mentored thousands of "Mighty Warriors" worldwide. Thank God this General of the Faith was willing to minister at the Levesque Assembly of God!

Our friends. Ministers far and wide. Pastors, Evangelists, Prophets, and Teachers who have continuously poured into our lives and ministry. So many great, powerful, anointed leaders, too numerous to name.

Our Church family. Churches, members, partners, family, and friends who believe in our ministry and allow us space and place to speak into their lives.

Drs. Stephen and Michelle Everett and their exceptional expertise and investment are integral to this project.

My wife. A mighty Prophet, Preacher, Teacher, and Psalmist in her own right. A beautiful and precious example of a Pastor's Wife.

My sons. Gracious, talented, anointed servants who have sacrificed time, talent, and substance to this ministry and this work.

# Contents

# Introduction

Blessed be the God and Father
of our Lord Jesus Christ, Who has blessed us
with every spiritual blessing
in the heavenly places in Christ.
~ Ephesians 1:3

## Welcome to *the Table!*

There is always something special for you at *the Table* of the Lord. Jesus took special effort and attention to prepare and provide the best for us. No detail has been overlooked. Nothing is missing, lacking, undone, or unfinished. No one could ever imagine the blessings, privileges, and benefits that await the child of God at **the Table.**

Fellowship and friendship with the Lord are so precious! The opportunity to abide in His Presence is like nothing else on earth. There is no better experience or expression. No comparison exists. He always offers us the very best. We are invited and given access to the most prestigious and blessed place. We have been offered the greatest gift. Truly, we have amazing access and a priceless invitation.

What have we done with this invitation? Have we responded to His invitation? Have we taken our place in Him?

1

This book will address the beauty and the glory of the opportunity to receive miraculous provision and fellowship from the Father. It is the goal of this project to show that God's good provision is for *you*. He cares!

He knows how to take good care of His children. He knows how to meet our every need. We are not forgotten, neglected, or forsaken. God's good provision is for you. He desires to give us life and life more abundantly.[1] He will always do exceedingly abundantly beyond all we can ask or think.[2]

In preparation for this work, I began to ask the Lord, "Why this book?" Below is the response I received from the Holy Spirit:

> *Why this book?* Because God said so.
>
> The printed word is so very important.
>
> Get it recorded...
>
> To be a blessing and a teaching tool;
>
> To be a solid and available resource;
>
> To guide and aid believers to trust, believe, and fellowship with God.

So, in agreement with Holy Spirit, let's go to *the Table!*

---

God's work done in God's way
will never lack God's supplies.
~ Hudson Taylor

2

Inspiration for *the Table*

# Take the First Step

Let us look to Jesus, the author and
finisher of our faith, who for the joy that was
set before Him endured the cross, despising
the shame, and is seated at the right hand of
the throne of God. ~ Hebrews 12:2

**God knows exactly where you are.** Do not let that statement startle or surprise you. It is not a scare tactic. God knows where we are, what we are going through, and everything we need, desire, or want. He knows how to deliver and provide those things in His perfect timing and way.

Let me introduce you to Purcell Church. A friend invited us to a revival service in Arkansas a few years ago. Many people have talked about country churches in the middle of nowhere. This church was, without a doubt, exactly that. Thank God for churches like this. Many modern-minded individuals often dismiss these out-of-the-way, off-the-beaten-path, old-time churches. But in doing so, they miss out on the simplicity of seeking God and serving Him, which is the first and foremost priority in these types of places. Several churches such as these have tremendously affected our family and ministry. Their legacy and heritage are vital, and I cannot thank God enough for them.

The first time we attended service at Purcell Church, it seemed we would never get there. It is in the country, down a long narrow road, and the only "neighbor" is an old cemetery next to the property. It was a simple old wooden building with nothing outstanding regarding its appearance. There was no parking lot, just a little grass along the gravel county road. As we walked in, we could feel the floor give slightly underneath our feet. When we got to our seats in one of the old wooden pews, the opposite end of the pew would rise as we sat down due to the uneven floor condition. However, none of this mattered as the spiritual climate and condition of the house were nothing like the physical condition or characteristics of the building. The atmosphere was supercharged with the Presence of God. The love and warmth of the people overwhelmingly made you feel welcome and right at home. Their desire was for a move of the Spirit of God.

Of course, this one-of-a-kind church would have to have a one-of-a-kind pastor to match! Pastor Miles was a perfect fit for Purcell Church. He loved these people very much and faithfully labored to the best of his ability. He desired, more than anything, the Presence of the Lord to touch these people and change their lives. I have never met anyone like him.

Just as the church was completely original and the Pastor was strikingly one of his own, it is to be expected that not just any Evangelist would have the privilege to preach behind this precious and unique pulpit. This was a task divinely selected and specifically prepared for Evangelist Linda Brewer. Sister Brewer is a powerful force full of God's anointing, power, wisdom, and Word. Her ministry is widely known and well-regarded. It is to be noted that God had strategically set in order a beautiful plan and specifically brought these people together for such a time and such a purpose. Thank God there are still ministers willing to go to places like this and boldly stand up and proclaim, "Thus saith the Lord."

The service was a very precious and special time in the Presence of the Lord. During the conclusion of the service, Sister Brewer began to minister, praying for various individuals who had responded to the moving of the Holy Spirit. Suddenly, her attention was drawn to me, and she quickly moved in our direction. First, Sister Brewer began to pray, then paused before boldly beginning to prophesy. As she obeyed God, what was said alarmed me. The first statement was different from what I expected or wanted to hear.

**"There's a book in you."**

A book? What do you mean? *In me?* I had known for quite some time that there were several projects God desired from us, but I never dreamed or expected a book was one of them. This was a great challenge and required a huge leap of faith. For a moment, this statement took my breath away. This idea seemed so out of reach. For sure, this was out of my comfort zone!

Of course, the Lord knew everything in my heart and all the thoughts swirling in my head. Then, as only the Holy Spirit can, the Lord graciously extended His comforting love and voice most beautifully. This kind, encouraging confirmation from the Lord through Sister Brewer has ministered to me many times ever since; she said, "I see all these stacks of files and things in your office. You have stacks of papers and files on your desk. They are all in different groupings. One stack here and another stack here. Each one is sorted and separated. The information— {all that} you have been sorting and gathering—is right before you." This was a perfect description of my office and desk. She was exactly right. This precious confirmation was an aid to help and encourage me to step up in faith and obedience to the assignment of the Lord.

As I began to seek the Lord, He brought many things to my remembrance. He brought clarity to what seemed and looked like confusion and brought order and priority to the work already begun. Now, it was my turn and responsibility to continue.

It is up to us to take the necessary steps of obedience. It is time for all of us to respond obediently in faith to what God has asked us to do. It is such a simple and beautiful concept. Just do whatever the Lord tells us to do.[3] Do not delay or become distracted. Tune out and turn off all the distractions and other voices. Do not make things more complicated than they are. Simplify things and walk in obedience. **Just do what Jesus says.**

There is nothing like a direct word from the Lord to impact our lives. He can change any situation with one word in less than a moment's notice. His Voice and His Presence make all the difference. So many times throughout the Bible, His intervention and inspiration totally and completely changed the course of nations. One inspired man or woman of God responding in obedience to His voice has made every difference in countless generations.

Inspiration is never far from us. God inspired the entirety of the Holy Bible. Every word is by direct inspiration from His Holy Spirit. *Inspiration is as simple as taking a deep breath.* It is as simple as leaning closer to the Lord Jesus Christ and intently listening to what His Word is speaking to us. The Spirit of God is always at work in the believer's life—always moving, speaking, and inspiring the children of God.

The dictionary defines inspiration as "an inspiring agent or influence, the quality or state of being inspired, the act of drawing in, a divine influence or action on a person believed to qualify him or her to receive and communicate sacred revelation."[4] According to 2 Timothy 3:16, "All Scripture is inspired by God." The entirety of His Word is divinely inspired. Every passage, every phrase, every word. There is nothing more valuable or more important than the Word of God. As we study His Holy Word, the Spirit of God speaks and reveals the truth of this precious, inspired Word. He brings constant revelation and inspiration to the devoted reader. Too often, people allow fear or other pressures to keep them from studying God's Word. Many are neglecting the best gift given to this world. His Word will inspire you in every area. Everything we need for life and godliness is available to us—it is all inside the Bible.[5]

At the time of our visit to Purcell Church, I had been in ministry for several years. In my years of service to the Lord, I have served in the Church in multiple capacities. My goal and desire were always to be a disciplined student of the Word of

God. As a Pastor, it is vital to receive inspiration from the Holy Spirit and His Word. As a son of God, receiving nourishment in His Presence is important. After submitting to His prompting and leading, I now recognize that He had prepared me for this assignment.

What does He desire from *you?* What are the assignments that He has pressed on your heart? Jump into His Word and engage in His Presence!

Maybe you did not have the kind of encounter and experience I had in this revival service, but I believe you do know the moment when God was calling you. Right now, at this moment, there is fresh revelation and inspiration for you. Do not allow the cares of this life to keep you from completing what God has given you.

He created you specifically for His purpose. He had the plan and the process in order before you were born. It was His desire for you to accomplish great things for His Kingdom and His glory. The God-given dreams and assignments designed for you can only be best fulfilled and carried out *by you.* That is why he gave it to you! He trusted the assignment with you. He selected, designed, created, and crafted you in His infinite wisdom and knowledge.

Get started today. Finish those projects. Do not allow your life to be a series of unfinished tasks. Do not bury those talents and giftings in the graveyard. Allow God to bring to completion what He has birthed in you. Think of it! What a privilege to be used by Him. What an honor to serve Him.

As you seek the Lord's direction, I firmly believe that this season of your life will be the most prosperous and fruitful you have ever experienced. I encourage you today to take the first step. Write the first song. Share that testimony. Teach the class. Preach the message. Together, let's take our seats at *the Table!*

---

Faith takes the first step
even when you don't see the whole staircase.
~ Martin Luther King, Jr.

You're Included at *the Table*

# Go! Preach the Word

Go therefore and make disciples of all
nations, baptizing them in the name of
the Father and of the Son and of the Holy
Spirit, teaching them to observe all things I
have commanded you. And remember, I am
with you always, even to the end of the age.
~ Matthew 28:19-20

**Every one of us has been selected** and commissioned to preach the gospel of Jesus Christ. As the call of God began to develop in my life, I had no idea of the fullness and the reality of what God was asking of me. I never intended to be involved in ministry, and it was especially not my plan or desire to be a full-time pastor. However, God had a completely different design and destiny!

As the call of God began to unfold in my life, I expected to serve God through music ministry. I planned to serve God from the piano and never be required to open my mouth to preach or teach. How wonderful our Lord is to us. How gracious and merciful He is. He allows us to grow into the anointing, grace, and destiny that is in our life. God knew that as a young Christian, I could not process all He had planned for my life. He was so patient in working with me. The Lord

15

was so kind and loving during every mishap and mistake. He continued to lead and guide me every single step of the way.

Let us be quick to respond to His call. Too often, we have refrained from fully obeying this command because most Christians fear the word *preach*. It is very interesting to note that this word is not included in Matthew's account of the Great Commission. However, without a doubt, preaching is highly imperative and necessary. Preaching has been misunderstood and misinterpreted for many years. In the church, we have made it into something that perhaps God never intended. Preaching has been confined to only what occurs behind a pulpit on a Sunday morning. It is so much more!

As we look at the words of Jesus in Matthew 28, there are several important action words—go, make, baptize, teach, and remember. Therefore, true biblical preaching requires *action!*

First, He said, *"Go."* Go tell. Go show. Go share. Go and encourage others. Go help someone. Go and testify what Jesus has done for you—*today!*

It is important to note that when God demanded us to "Go," the command was to go beyond all borders into every nation. We cannot confine the gospel to our own area or comfort zone. Remove all limits. Remove all hesitations. Move beyond our preferences. Let's walk in total love and obedience to the call of the Father. Let's go where He sends us to go!

The mandate of God is for His gospel to go into ALL the earth. Nations are calling. People worldwide are hungry for the things of God, and they do not even realize it. They are searching and reaching for answers. We know **the** answer: Jesus! It is

16

up to us to be bold and not only open our mouths to share but put action in our steps—get on our feet and take the glorious news of Jesus to this lost and hurting world. Through Him, we are going to reach this world!

Second, He said, *"Make."* This reminds me of the command God gave humanity when He created them. He instructed them to "be fruitful and multiply."[6] God wants His Kingdom to advance and expand. He wants us to be about His business—teaching, training, instructing, and making disciples.[7] The process of making a disciple is not instantaneous work. It is involved in the lives of others. It takes time and investment to do this. It is an ongoing active process. We must be willing to walk beside others and build relationships with them as they journey with Christ. As we walk with them, we can *teach* and train them in the ways of the Lord.

This seems like such a daunting and difficult task, but Jesus reminded them and His Word reminds us that He makes this possible. *Remember.* He promised that He was always with us. Jesus remains with us throughout all the ages. Furthermore, He promised He would give us power through the Holy Ghost to accomplish all He has called us to do fully. Stop thinking that this is only a job for the "Preacher." We are all preachers! All of us have a testimony. It is time to open our mouths and share the good things our good God has done.

Paul states in Romans 10 that we hear about Jesus through preachers. Thank God, there was a preacher that was willing to share with me! Thank God that someone was willing to tell me that God loved me. In fact, He loved me so much that He sent

17

Jesus for me. God loves you so much that He the made way for you. He has provided the only perfect way for you and me to be reconciled to Him. Jesus is the Way, the Truth, and the Life, and in Him, we have access to God the Father.[8] Through Jesus, we have eternal life. Because of Jesus, we have a seat at *the Table.*

Stop believing the ridiculous, tired, and twisted lies of the enemy. There is a place and an assignment for you, and you are the only one that can properly fulfill the God-crafted assignment and task specifically destined for you. There is a place for you. **You are included.** Therefore, open your mouth and proclaim the good news of God. You can do ALL *things* through Christ Who strengthens you![9] Maybe, one of those *things* is *preaching.* You may not ever stand behind a pulpit, but you have a message, and it is imperative that you share that message with the audience God intended for you to have.

Don't allow the enemy of fear and intimidation to keep you from sharing the gospel. It is important to recognize some of the lies the enemy has been propagating so that you (we) stop falling for his tactics. One of the first lies he promoted is that ministry is only for the elite or the qualified. Of course not! All believers are called to minister. The only requirement is to have a relationship with Jesus and a walk with God. Out of that walk with God, there will be constant and continuous testimonies of His goodness and His power working in your life. Then, you open your mouth and speak forth His Word. Share what He has done for you. You are very capable of telling somebody about Jesus. We have the mandate to tell people about Him.

He has called all of us to be His witnesses. Once He calls us, we are then qualified. He will equip and mature us as we surrender to His call and obediently walk with Him.

A second popular lie is quite similar. People have assumed that church leaders are the only ones who should minister. Too many church attendees leave all the ministry's responsibilities and duties to the church leaders. Dear God, no! No wonder many of our pastors and church leaders are exhausted and overwhelmed. Too many in the body have accepted this fallacy as truth. Your pastor needs your help—he or she cannot be everywhere at the same time. You have input and connections to people and places that they do not. You can go where they cannot go. God has strategically placed you in that spot and assignment to witness and minister to those around you. It is the will and plan of God for the whole body to function as He designed it. We need each other. In 1 Corinthians 12, it is very clear that the entire body is necessary *every day* for the work of the ministry. We must work together in and for His Kingdom. We need each other! Doing so is our joy, honor, duty, and privilege!

The third lie is that someone else will do it instead of me. In other words, someone else will take care of it. Someone else can do it better. This is very dangerous and deadly thinking. It has caused much devastation and damage. The enemy attempts to convince believers that someone else is more qualified or capable. He may try to get you to compare yourself with someone else, which the Bible says is not wise.[10] God has faith in you to do the work He has called you to. God does not make

19

mistakes; if He has called you, He has more than qualified and equipped you to succeed. With Him, you can do it! With God, ALL things are possible!

The last lie of the devil is one many people have fallen for. He wants you to think and believe you are not worthy or good enough. The devil wants you to accept that you have not lived a life good enough to minister to others. By all means, if that were true, no one would ever be or would have ever been able to minister or share the gospel. Many examples in the Word of God reveal that God used imperfect people. Thank God, He still does. We all need Jesus! Every person is flawed. All of us have made mistakes and missteps. We all need forgiveness. We all need the mercy and grace of God. Jesus has made you able. You can do the task. Because of Him, you can testify of His goodness and tell His story. In Christ, you are more than enough! He has made you worthy. You are the righteousness of God in Christ Jesus![11]

Jesus wants you at His Table!

---

If God is your partner, make your plans BIG!
~ D. L. Moody

# Go! Reach the World

How then shall they call on Him in whom
they have not believed? And how shall they
believe in Him of whom they have not heard?
And how shall they hear without a preacher?
And how shall they preach unless they are
sent? As it is written: "How beautiful are the
feet of those who preach the gospel of peace,
who bring good news of good things!"
~ Romans 10:14-15

**God has greatly equipped us** to reach His world! Through His strength, we can accomplish every task at hand! Our calling and assignment are much bigger than we could ever imagine. We must reach our full potential and complete the work God ordained for His people. Let us begin to move with the Holy Spirit as He guides us to reach this world for Jesus.

It is understood that Jesus commanded His disciples to go into ALL the world.[12] The heart of God is to "Go." We see the Lord coming to His people throughout the Word of God. He desires fellowship with us. Our greatest desire should be fellowship with Him. The Bible is full of this pattern of operation. God always makes it a priority to minister to His people. He has always made His Presence available. He has given and allowed the most gracious and merciful access to Himself through His Son, Jesus. What a privilege! What an honor of incomparable joy! Nothing is better than sitting at His feet, seeking His face, and hearing His voice. There is no better way to live!

I pray that His heart, desire, love, compassion, and compelling Spirit will be our driving force. May He put us in hyper drive, equipping and accelerating us to reap His harvest! Lord, move your Church into action! Mobilize your Body into an actively engaged response. Empower your people for your purpose and glory! Give us ears to hear, eyes to see, hearts to love, and feet to GO!

Always remember that the ministry is God's idea. It is a gift that He has provided for our benefit. First, God gave the world Jesus.[13] Without Him, there is no life, truth, or hope. There is no ministry without Him. Jesus came to this world to save and redeem us with His blood. He has established His Church and revealed us as His Body.

God also gave gifts to the church. These gifts are leaders. They are purposed to equip, strengthen, and build *the Body* for the work of the ministry, to mature and develop His Body into the full capacity God desires.[14] As His Body, we have a great task before us, but with Christ, we can do the work and accomplish the task.

It is so important to keep proper focus and our motives pure. Why do we do what we do? Why on earth are we here? We are here to serve Jesus. We are here to live for Him. We give our lives for His service to His purpose according to His command and design. Jesus said, "Seek first the Kingdom of

God and His righteousness."[15] To seek His Kingdom, we must be about our Father's business. To seek His Righteousness, we must submit and obey His commands in His Word. God has work for us to do. He desires us to produce fruit and bring increase in our life actively.

> I urge you therefore, brothers, by the mercies of God, that you present your bodies as a living sacrifice, holy, and acceptable to God, which is your reasonable service of worship. Do not be conformed to this world, but be transformed by the renewing of your mind, that you may prove what is the good and acceptable and perfect will of God. (Romans 12:1-2)

The tasks and assignments God calls us to are so vitally important. God has placed them upon our hearts, assigning them for both our benefit and the corporate benefit of the body. It is our most reasonable and simple act of worship, dedication, and service to God. We must respond in total obedience to His commands.

God often challenges us. His Spirit is always stretching us. He is always reaching out to us. He is ever bidding us to come unto Him. It is our precious opportunity to draw close to God. That is the beautiful part of our maturing and growing process—to grow, we must step out in obedience and faith.

In the book of James, the Bible says that "faith by itself, if it has no works, is dead."[16] As God began dealing with me regarding this book, it seemed to be too much of a daunting and challenging task. It took a long time for me to surrender to the assignment. Thank God, He is patient. Thank God for His forgiveness when we delay responding to His instructions. They never change. The call never goes away. God is ever faithful to continue drawing us. He is so merciful as He patiently waits for us to put our faith into action and to get down to His business.

The projects that God placed in your heart are important. Do not linger any longer. Take it from me: God does not ask someone to do the impossible without His help. There is no such thing as impossible in His Kingdom.[17] When we connect with His plan and His project, what blessings and benefits flow into our life! Oh, what tremendous fruit will abound as we submit to His work! As we allow the Holy Spirit to flow through us, working His plan and assignment, great fruit will begin to flourish. The harvest will unfold right before our eyes. It is His delight to bring these things to pass in our life. God has great plans for all His children. May His divine and distinct purpose be more clearly revealed to us more and more every day.

I am totally persuaded that God really wants us to succeed. It is His idea that His children not only bear fruit but that we are extremely fruitful. The fruit that exists in our life is completely for His glory. These projects, these plans, and these works are God's ideas. He wants them to be completed and developed more than we do. He wants us to understand the importance of the completion of the work. As our Heavenly Father, it is His great delight to get His projects into our hearts and hands. Then, we must sow them out of our hands into the lives and hearts of others around us. Until the work is completed, it cannot bring the fullness of blessing or multiplication in the Kingdom. Let's get the seed into the field. His projects will always produce fruit. When we grasp the goals, plans, and desires He has for us, what an incredible difference will be made in our lives and those we encounter. He wants you to succeed! However, **we never succeed until we proceed.**

A minister once said that graveyards, cemeteries, and mausoleums contain the largest collection of unfinished and unpublished masterpieces. Lord, let us not be guilty of taking your Truth, Light, and revelation to our grave. Let us speak, write, compose, draw, develop, and manifest the projects you have birthed within us. Let us not hold back, stay still, or keep silent. Let us get it completed, published, and recorded.

I want this present generation and the next generation to benefit from God's blessing in my life. Come on! Write the book! Value what God has given and birthed in you. Spend time with God. Let Him give you the vision, the insight, and the revelation. Write it down and record it. You're *your* "God story." Someone needs to run with it![18] Do not let your life be a series of unfinished projects.

**God values the written word.** His Word is by far and above the single most valuable treasure in the world, both now and in the age to come. God ensured that His Word was forever recorded and preserved for ALL time. It will never pass away.[19] God's books, articles, songs, and other materials are also important. They are such a blessing to those who receive them. God's projects given to God's people shed light and bring insight into His Word. We must not neglect our assignments.

The beauty of a book is that it will continue to produce fruit far beyond, above, and long after the author or contributor transitions to heaven. Growth, multiplication, harvest, distribution, and application will continue as people read, view, hear, and distribute the material. Our responsibility is to preserve and record the knowledge and revelation that the Holy Spirit has deposited within us. We must not take this precious and priceless Truth to the grave unspoken and unwritten. Now is the time to respond quickly and obediently to the Holy Spirit's promptings. Those gifts, leadings, and promptings are vital. They can truly make all the difference in someone's life. A seed not sown never produces. However, every seed sown always produces.

Make the commitment today. Completely submit and surrender! Enjoy the process. Let's reach this world! Preach, teach, and make disciples now!

---

Without the assistance of the Divine Being…
I cannot succeed.
With that assistance, I cannot fail.
~ Abraham Lincoln

# People are Ready

*O Lord, you are so good, so ready to forgive,*
*so full of unfailing love for all who ask for your*
*help. ~ Psalm 86:5 (NLT)*

**There has never been a season or time such as this.** It would be very tempting to think there is no hope for our world. It could be very easy for us to look around at the condition of our world and give up. We must never quit. God has made a beautiful way for all of us! He has a perfect plan. Now is the time for the people of God to unashamedly preach the Word and proclaim His Truth. Yes, it is time to be instant in season and out of season.[20] As people of God's Word, we must live and walk in His Light.

Is this world a dark place? Is it time to repent and turn to God? YES! Without a doubt, this world is crying out for deliverance. Entire people groups are looking and longing for answers. The nations of this earth are waiting and ready. The call of God is at hand. Someone is expecting and waiting on you. There is still room at *the Table!* God has called us. He has equipped and commissioned us to go. It is time to respond in obedience and active faith.

Friend, it is a blessed and beautiful thing to spread the gospel of the Lord Jesus! "How beautiful are the feet of messengers who bring good news."[21] According to Strong's Concordance, in Isaiah 52:7 and Romans 10:15, the word beautiful refers to "becoming, fitting, or appropriate." It contains the notion of belonging to the right hour or season.[22]

It is not only a beautiful and glorious thing to spread the gospel, but how appropriate and timely it is for us to be about our Heavenly Father's business. Jesus asks us to "go out into the highways and hedges and compel them to come in that my house may be filled."[23] **We are to speak to as many as we shall find.**

Worldwide, individuals are searching diligently for something authentic and different. No longer are they satisfied with someone's traditions or regulations; they are looking for what only Jesus can provide. Man-made, man-crafted, and man-controlled religions will not satisfy the needs and desires of this world. These twisted and corrupted religious systems have become the number one method of mass destruction in our world today.

This is why the gospel is so beautiful. Jesus and His Church are the only ones to provide answers and satisfaction! I'm speaking of *His Church,* which the Holy Spirit completely controls. His Church where His Word is boldly proclaimed and spoken in God's love. His Church—where His people are set free, healed, delivered, and anointed. His Church where the saints humble themselves by seeking God and experiencing the glory of His Presence. This is what we need today!

Hell may have many plans for humanity. The spirit of death has many snares. For those in the world, great darkness covers this present world system. However, the Church will always prevail! The Church of Jesus Christ is triumphant because **Christ never fails.** Because He will not fail, we will not fail as we remain in Him. This is why Jesus promised, "He would build His Church, and the gates of hell will not prevail against it!"[24]

From God's perspective, these are not days of total gloom on the earth. Stop singing the devil's song and start proclaiming the Word of the Lord. His Church with His Word will prevail. His will shall be done, and He will accomplish what He desires.

These are the days of His glory. These are the days when He is speaking to and through His Church. Boldly proclaim what He has spoken to you. Share the insight and the knowledge that the Holy Spirit has given you. *Stop holding back.* So many people around you are waiting to hear what God has given you to say. Your family is counting on you. Your neighbor is counting on you. Your co-workers are counting on you. Step up and speak up today.

The return of the Lord Jesus is coming very soon. It is so much sooner than any of us think. In Matthew chapter 24 and Luke chapter 17, Jesus mentions the conditions of the end-time last days' world. "Just as it was in the days of Noah," Jesus said regarding the conditions of the world.[25]

Thinking about the reference of Jesus to the days of Noah, the Bible records in Genesis 6 that wickedness, sin, and evil had completely penetrated the hearts of the people. Every thought, desire, and imagination of man was perverse. It is much the same today. This world is in great darkness, and the standard of the world will continue to degrade and deteriorate. However, amid such darkness and evil, the precious Light of Jesus shines so brightly.

We must let His light shine in these days! We must remain faithful to Him. Look for a moment at the life of Noah. Amid such tremendously widespread evil, Noah was a man of faith. He was a man who was completely devoted to God. In Genesis 6:8, the Bible says that Noah was a righteous man. It says he found favor with the Lord.

Further, it also says he was blameless and walked in close fellowship with God.[26] When we jump ahead to the book of Hebrews, some fascinating details are revealed regarding the life and faith of Noah. He walked with God. He obeyed God. God gave Noah advanced insight, knowledge, and warning regarding future things that had never been seen before. Examine the following translations of Hebrews 11:7:

> …being divinely warned about things not yet seen. (MEV)

> …being forewarned by God concerning events of which as yet there was no visible sign. (AMPC)

> He obeyed God, who warned him about things that had never happened before. (NLT)

Faith opened Noah's heart to receive revelation and warnings from God about what was coming, even things that had never been seen. (TPT)

In these times, our relationship with God, like Noah, can give us advanced knowledge of what will come. We can be ready, and we must be ready! Time is drawing near, and the day of salvation is at hand.

There is no better investment than the Kingdom of God. The vision is to reach the entire world. The goal is the advancement of the Kingdom of God in every nation. Our hearts should beat with the desire to bring the good news of our good God to the very ends of the earth. Our intention should be to share ALL that Jesus has done for us. That is the glorious beauty of the gospel. Jesus, the glorified King, is the same as He has always been. He will forever remain the same. His complete and finished work is available now for all! What He has done for me, He will do for you. He is an awesome, mighty, powerful God worthy of all our praise. He's the answer to creation's cry. Every part of this creation calls out to hear more about Him.

Hurting people are searching everywhere to find peace. People are desperately seeking answers to their problems. In these days of deceit and deception, it is imperative that we, as ambassadors and soldiers of Christ, rise to the call and challenge before us. It is time for us to be fully equipped and armed with the whole armor of God. It is time for God's Word and His Truth to flow from our entire being. This is the season for the unction of the Holy Ghost. Let us always be ready to give the answer! The answer is always Jesus! Jesus is the only answer to every question, struggle, and situation in life. He is the Way, the only and absolute Truth. He is our Life.[27] Through Him and Him alone can we do ALL things.[28]

How do we answer this call? The response of Isaiah is completely appropriate in this case, "Here am I, Lord, send me."[29] When people reach out, let us be quick to respond as the Spirit of God provides opportunity.

The harvest is huge. People are ready for the gospel. Jesus said it truly is plentiful. It is time for us to get into the field and put our hands to work. It is time for us to share and show the love of God every day. Someone is waiting on you. Let's bring as many as possible to *the Table* with us!

---

We are never defeated, unless we give up on God.
~ Ronald Reagan

You're Welcome at *the Table*

# A Testimony of a Table

But my God shall supply your every need
according to His riches in glory by Christ
Jesus. ~ Philippians 4:19

**Things in this earthly life do not stay the same.** When I think back to my childhood, wonderful memories flood my mind. Our home was blessed. The love of God was ever-present in our home, and I never wondered if my family loved me. There was no doubt. Still, to this day, I can remember many times sitting around our family table. There were only three of us, Mom, Dad, and me. I remember those times, and I remember the table. Not only were there precious and special times spent around our home dining table. There were also very priceless and treasured times at my grandparents' tables. I am so grateful for these rare treasures, now cherished memories of great value stored in my heart. It is nice to reminisce and reflect on the blessing of God and to thank Him for the legacy of love and faith that He established and preserved in my family.

So yes, it is true, things in this earthly life do not stay the same. The only constant and the only stability is the Lord Jesus Christ! He is the same yesterday, today, and forever.[30] Thank God, He will never change, and neither will His Word. Absolutely every circumstance and situation is subject to change. As we serve God growing closer to Him and maturing in Christ, improvement and advancement come. It may seem like the darkness will never lift. It may seem like the dawn will not arrive, but I assure you, the sun will rise. God has not forgotten His own. He has not forgotten you. The brilliant and beautiful light of Jesus is always shining. God is always at work, and He always has not only a plan but a GREAT PLAN! He has something good in store for you and knows how to deliver it to you at the perfect time.

One of the greatest blessings of being in the Lord's Church and serving His people is to witness His transforming and delivering power in each other's lives. The Bible is full of God's miraculous record. Our churches have multiple testimonies and accounts of healings, deliverances, salvations, miracles, and demonstrations of God's mighty power. Again, our God is always working. He is always providing. God is always making the Way. He is leading and guiding our steps, and we can completely, confidently trust Him!

In 2012, I had the distinct and great privilege of fellowshipping with one of the greatest gospel singers of our time, Evangelist Nancy Harmon. Like so many, I loved watching her sing and minister on the Trinity Broadcasting Network. Her program, "The Love Special," aired on TBN for over forty years and was, without a doubt, a ground-breaking program. She was among the first to regularly air such a powerful, Spirit-filled musical program. Nancy and her team consistently ministered with boldness under the anointing and unction of the Holy Spirit. To know Evangelist Harmon was to love and appreciate her. She truly walks with a mighty anointing and great integrity. It is (and has always been) a tremendous joy and privilege to witness her ministry in person or on air. Anytime Evangelist Harmon entered the room, the entire atmosphere would change. She walks with God. When she opens her mouth, the anointing of God fills the room. I remember the first time Bill Gaither included her in one of his Homecoming videos—everything changed. There was a tangible and marked difference in the sound and in the level of praise. The same happened when Sister Nancy was invited to minister on the SonLife Broadcasting Network. There was a mighty shift in the service.

God gifted and blessed Nancy Harmon with an anointed voice and an incredible ability to write Gospel music and lyrics. However, her precious sacrifice and investment in the young people she personally mentored and included in her ministry team may perhaps be what will go down in God's history as her greatest accomplishment and investment in the Body of Christ. Sister Nancy selflessly shared herself, her ministry, her life, and her platforms with the young men and women willing to travel and minister with her. She invested so much into each one. As a Pastor, I was blessed to witness as she did this in our local church and our family. Her ministry is so precious to me, and I am eternally grateful for her gift in my life and my family's life.

In the Spring of 2012, my oldest son wanted to travel with Evangelist Harmon as a "Mighty Warrior." She accepted him into the program and allowed him to join her that year as she traveled during the summer months. In preparation for the up-coming tour, we enjoyed lunch one day, and she began to share a beautiful testimony regarding one of her team members.

She told us the story of Lori Bird. If you ever watched "The Love Special," you most likely heard Lori preach or sing. She was an amazing vocalist and preacher. Like our son, Lori was another of the thousands of young people that traveled and ministered with Nancy Harmon. Her story was powerful, but her childhood was very sad. Lori had grown up abused and mistreated. She did not have a childhood filled with love and hope. Her father was cruel, and she was often mistreated, un-loved, and abused.

This young girl, neglected and mistreated, would do her best to sneak out of her room early on Sunday mornings and watch Christian Television while the other family members slept. Christian programs were not allowed in her home, and she would be punished even more if they caught her. Her father often would withhold food from her, and during such punishment, he would only allow her to eat cornflakes with water.

Even so, she risked the punishment for the hope and fulfillment that came to her heart from watching the Christian television programing. One of her favorite programs to watch was the Rex Humbard Family. He was one of the pioneers of tel-evangelism and media ministry. Rex Humbard was an amazing visionary. He and his wife, Maude Aimee, had several children and the whole family sang, celebrated, and ministered together with love and exuberance. This intrigued Lori greatly, and she strongly desired to be a part of such a family.

She would recount the story that as a nine-year-old child, she would pray, "If I could just sit at Rex Humbard's table, this wouldn't happen." It was such a desire of her heart to feel love and acceptance. She knew the minister's table would have love, tenderness, and kindness. She knew that he would not treat his children that way. She knew that if she were a part of this family, she would not be forced to eat cereal with water. And in her heart, she knew God would not treat His children that way.

Several years passed, and Lori joined the Nancy Harmon Ministries team, where she began ministering on the Love Special. The Lord was greatly blessing Lori, and the time arrived that she got her first apartment. Lori and her roommate had many friends who shared their excitement and were eager to help. As others had done, a mutual friend contacted Lori and wanted to help furnish this apartment. She offered her a table. Lori would soon learn that this was not just any table...

> "A few days later, I casually mentioned to Sarah and Lori that Maude Aimee Humbard had once owned the table we had given to them. It was then that I learned the story of Lori's sad childhood. Her father was abusive in every way. He became angry if he caught Lori listening to Christian TV Sunday mornings, so Lori would sneak down the stairs of their home to turn the volume low and sit close to the TV to watch Rex, Maude Aimee, and the family. She prayed

many times that someday she would be able to sit at *the table* of this beautiful family and belong to a family that offered so much love, acceptance, and security."[31]

You see, the table had made its way from the possession of the Humbards to Mrs. Sally Burton Vann. Sally had served in the Humbard's ministry, and at a time when she and her husband needed furniture for their apartment, Sister Humbard had blessed her with this precious table. *And now, it had made it's way into Lori's life.*

God had been at work the entire time! He was moving in a remarkable way behind the scenes, and His plan was unfolding even when it seemed to be unnoticed. God had answered her prayers! Not only had He graciously placed her into a ministry family that treasured and loved her, but He gave her a table from a ministry that had been such an encouragement and blessing to her young life. He had not forgotten her prayer, and He had not failed to provide for her. *God hears every prayer and knows every desire of our hearts. He is always working on our behalf.*

Let us never underestimate the power of such a gift. Let us never fail to listen closely as the Holy Spirit speaks and encourages us to give to others. How precious is a seed that we can sow into someone's life? What a blessing! What a harvest! What a celebration. The gifts that God gives to us are blessings that keep on giving and keep on blessing. It is a beautiful cycle of the faithfulness and goodness of God.

40

---

When you focus on being a blessing, God makes sure that you are always blessed in abundance.
~ Joel Osteen

# An Opportunity at a Table

And when Jesus reached the place, He looked
up and said to him, Zacchaeus, hurry and
come down; for I must stay at your house
today. ~ Luke 19:5 (AMPC)

**An invitation to intimacy is readily available to us.** The opportunity for fellowship is available to us as children of God. Some of the best times during a worship service are the moments near the conclusion of the service when the opportunity is given to sit back and linger in the Presence of the Lord. There have been many times when His Presence was so rich and powerful that no one desired to move or even make a sound. This type of experience has often been called a *holy hush*. There is something significant and meaningful when you allow yourself to stop and press into the Lord's Presence. It is a tragic tendency of religion to strip away moments such as this. These times of intimacy with the Lord are vital in our walk with Him. When we are willing to lay our agenda down and simply sit at the feet of Jesus, there is no better place we could ever be.

We have this beautiful opportunity every day of our life. We have a Divine invitation to fellowship, and God desires a relationship with His own. We are able and allowed to visit and communicate with our Heavenly Father. Our relationship with

43

Jesus is real and vital. He is a personal Savior. He is a personal Lord. He has provided us with beautiful access to His precious Presence. Time spent with Him is so very priceless and special to us. This time and relationship are much more than a ritualistic religious experience or encounter.

It is time to begin enjoying our relationship with Him. It is time to walk fully in His joy and embrace His Presence. We can realize a constant move of the power of the Holy Ghost. He is readily available to all who will receive Him. We have a wonderful Lord Who has given us such gracious, perfect, and beautiful gifts!

We need to enjoy the fellowship God has given to us with each other. Over the course of my life and ministry, I have had some amazing privileges and honors. I have been blessed to sit across the table from some wonderful men and women of God. God has provided some miraculous connections only possible because of His great mercy and grace. I have been blessed to sit with famous musicians both in the world and in the church.

I recognize that it is God Who has given me the grace and favor to sit with popular Evangelists, denominational leaders, and heads of large ministries. It is always a privilege to listen and glean wisdom and experience from those who have walked with God and experienced His great power in their lives. There is always something valuable to be learned and discovered while fellowshipping with such leaders.

God has also blessed our ministry with some of His finest servants. Our churches are filled with many giants of the faith. Their names may not be broadly known, but their faith and dedication to the Lord have been a mighty example to count-less lives. All these people have been brought to ***the Table*** for the entire body's benefit! We can benefit and learn from each other.

It is time to plug into the connection and take advantage of the relationships God has placed in our lives. We must build, invest, strengthen, and develop relationships with one anoth-er. We are connected for a purpose. We are connected for the Kingdom. We are connected for His glory. Let us enjoy our time together and our time with Him! It is a blessing. It is time for us to open up to one another and begin sharing the Word God has revealed in us. God is strategically putting us together at His Table, and we are serving Him together.

We have a precious opportunity to sit with Him and each other at His Table. He has invited us to intimacy with Him. He has offered us this divine fellowship. This is a precious oppor-tunity that we should never take for granted. He has prepared a great table for us. He is preparing a wonderful place for us. He is waiting to receive us. Let us act on this invitation today!

---

I want the whole Christ for my Savior,
the whole Bible for my book,
the whole Church for my fellowship,
and the whole world for my mission field.
~ John Wesley

45

# A Place at *the Table*

Jesus answered him, "Before Philip called you,
when you were under the fig tree, I saw you."
~ John 1:48

**We must slow down and dedicate ourselves to the most important priority.** It is very easy to become busy and so focused on the requirements before us that we fail to realize the importance of the Lord's Presence. Jesus has offered us such a priceless and precious gift. He has a place for us at His Table. It is a place of intimacy and relationship. It is a place of security, peace, hope, and strength. He has prepared a place much better than any other destination. The banquet that He has spread before us is ours for the taking. We can participate now. We can partake now. His hand is extended to us. His invitation is waiting.

Jesus is looking for you! He sees you right now. His invitation is for you, and Jesus desires you to join Him. He desires to touch your life and your heart. The Lord wants to transform your life into a life that is according to His will and His purpose. He wants great things for your life. He has a great purpose for you with great plans. His thoughts toward you are good! They are thoughts of peace.[32] God is searching throughout the earth, looking for people to strengthen and bless. He looks for His children whose hearts are pure before Him.[33] He knows where you are and is ready and waiting to help you. God is our very present help in times of trouble and our refuge in times of need, and we will not fear![34] He is with us.

There is a place at His Table for us! Let's take our seats with Him. Think for a moment about the lives of many people in the Bible. There are some beautiful examples of men and women like us who decided to take that seat. The great **hall of faith** (in Hebrews 11) is a great list of those that, despite challenges, difficulties, mistakes, sin, failure, death, and much more, continued to hold onto that seat with the heavenly Father. Nothing pulled them away. They were determined to persevere through every trial and distraction. No one could ever cause them to turn away from that fellowship and relationship with the Lord. The New Testament is full of men and women who flocked to Jesus and refused to leave His side. His great love drew them and kept them in His glorious Presence. Right now, you and I have the exact same opportunity to drop it all and run to His side. Let us fall before Him and stay at His feet.

How blessed we are! We have a place at His Table. He has invited and included us. We do not sit at the servant's table; we are included at the Master's table.

A woman of Canaan encountered Jesus in Matthew 15. She was pleading with Jesus to heal her daughter. Even the disciples asked Jesus to send her away, but she had such faith and trust in Him that she would not give up. She was willing to eat the crumbs that fell from the table. However, that was not what was necessary or required. She was offered a place at the Table that day. Grace and mercy were extended to her. Her daughter was healed.

The prodigal son (in Luke 15) found himself in a terrible situation. He had made some drastic and terrible decisions, and the consequences of sinful and wicked living caught up with him. Thank God he came back to the soundness of mind. He was willing to return to his Father's house as a servant. Again, this was not the case, and His Father welcomed him with open arms. He ran to meet his son and accepted him as if he had never left. It was a glorious and victorious return.

It is likewise a glorious and victorious return when we are determined to run home to our heavenly Father! We must neither eat under the table nor at the servant's table. We do not have to eat crumbs or leftovers. We may feast with Him at His Table! His best is waiting for us!

He sees you, and He loves you. He is searching; He is waiting. Come to *the Table*!

---

He wants you all to Himself to put His loving,
Divine arms around you.
~ Charles Stanley

# The Privilege is Yours

# It Has Been Given to You

Then He took the bread, and when He had
given thanks, He broke it and gave it to them,
saying, "This is My body which is given for you.
Do this in remembrance of Me."
~ Luke 22:19

**Remember Who your source is!** People are never your source. Your job is different from your source. God and God alone is your source! He is our perfect Provider. God has provided our every need according to His vast, plenteous, never-ending riches in Christ Jesus![35] God is my source, and He always provides. God's good provision is for you!

> Bless the Lord, O my soul, and all that is within me, bless His holy name. Bless the Lord, O my soul, and forget not all His benefits, who forgives all your iniquities, who heals all your diseases, who redeems your life from the pit, who crowns you with lovingkindness and tender mercies, who satisfies your mouth with good things, so that your youth is renewed like the eagle's. (Psalm 103:1-5)

"Forget not ALL His benefits!" God has given us so much! He has blessed us with so many good things. In fact, the Lord blesses us over and over every day. He has new mercies available every morning. He "daily loads us with benefits."[36]

Here are just a few of the many examples of how God miraculously provided for His people throughout the Word:

- He provided a donkey for Jesus.
- He provided locusts and wild honey for John the Baptist.
- He provided (and continues to provide) seed to the Sower.
- He fed Elijah by sending birds with food.
- He consistently provided manna for the Children of Israel.
- God provided water in the desert and meat for His people.
- He fed the multitudes during the earthly ministry of Jesus.

Time and time again, God always provides for His children. He is a faithful God. He is our Rewarder. We can completely trust Him at all times in every season and during any circumstance regarding whatever situation. He is our great Provider. Our good God knows how to get good things into our hands!

> I will provide grass in your fields for your livestock, that you may eat and be full. (Deuteronomy 11:15)

But my God shall supply your every need according to His riches in glory by Christ Jesus. (Philippians 4:19)

How much more will your Father who is in heaven give good things to those who ask Him! (Matthew 7:11)

Consider the ravens: They neither sow nor reap, they have neither storehouses nor barns. Yet God feeds them. How much more valuable are you than birds? (Luke 12:24)

If God so clothes the grass, which today is in the field and tomorrow is thrown into the oven, how much more will He clothe you? (Luke 12:28)

The Lord is my shepherd; I shall not want. (Psalm 23:1)

I have been young, and now am old; yet I have not seen the righteous forsaken, nor their offspring begging bread. (Psalm 37:25)

He truly cares and takes great care of His own! He knows our every need even before we ask. He has provided everything we need. It is our responsibility to receive what He has freely provided. Accept His precious gifts.

Put in place the grace, love, and mercy He has so generously and liberally supplied. There will never be a need that He has not already completely met in Christ Jesus. Jesus taught in Matthew 7 and Luke 12 that God has clothed the lilies and fed the sparrows. Since He has done this, will He not SO MUCH MORE take care of us? Let us not be of little faith. Let us realize how good He is. Let us trust Him more!

It is so much easier to accept God. It is so much easier to believe Him with child-like precious faith. It is so very wonderful to surrender, submit and trust Him. He is our good Father. He is our gracious and merciful Lord. He knows how to give us good gifts and enjoys blessing our life with His gifts and provision. His children will not be beggars. We will not depend on anyone or anything else. He has totally and completely provided everything we will ever need and ever have needed.

God has given us His greatest Gift. That is the Gift of Jesus. He loved us so much that He gave Jesus to us. He offered His one and only Son to redeem and purchase us. There will never be a greater Gift than this.

In Jesus, He gave us EVERYTHING!

---

We can be certain that God will give us the strength and resources we need to live through any situation in life that he ordains. The will of God will never take us where the grace of God cannot sustain us.
~ Billy Graham

# Do Not Despise the Wait

Wait on the Lord, be strong, and
may your heart be stout; wait on the Lord.
~ Psalm 27:14

**It is a beautiful and beneficial blessing to wait on the Lord.** Do not fall victim to the trap and deception of impatience. Patience is very good for us. There is a tremendous blessing that always comes to those that wait on the Lord. The Bible tells us that we have need of patience.[37] Why would we ever rebel against something our Lord tells us we need? The Strong's Concordance defines patience as cheerful or hopeful endurance.[38]

> For you need patience, so that after you have done the will of God, you will receive the promise. (Hebrews 10:36)

> Wait on the Lord and He will save you. (Proverbs 20:22)

> But those that wait upon the Lord shall renew their strength; they shall mount up with wings as eagles, they shall run and not be weary, and they shall walk and not faint. (Isaiah 40:31)

Patience produces steadfastness, yields consistency, proves constant, and develops endurance. There is great strength and blessing in waiting with God as He moves in our life. As our Shepherd, Leader, and Provider, He knows exactly what and when we need it. We often forget that God's great purpose involves much more than our preferences and desires. Currently, we cannot see the entire picture of the plan of God. However, as we wait, His plan will unfold perfectly and precisely. In His timing with His direction, there are no mistakes or missteps. When walking in step and sync with Him, we do not have to backtrack and correct our wrong turns.

It is so vital to be led every moment of every day of our life by the Holy Spirit. We must learn to listen closely to His voice. We must yield to His every direction and His every Word. Every letter that the Lord Jesus sent to the churches (via John, in the book of Revelation) included the same instruction, "He who has an ear, let him hear what the Spirit says to the churches." His Spirit will always lead and guide us into ALL Truth.[39]

**His Spirit is speaking. His Spirit is guiding. We must patiently listen and follow.**

Do not despise, reject or neglect this process that God is working in you. Just because there may be a delay does not mean God has denied you. **The answer is on the way.** God is never late. He is always exactly on time. However, it is His time, not ours! We can trust His timing.

It is in the waiting where the proper preparations are presented, preserved, and perfected. This is precious time, and your character will be developed. You will mature as you stand on the Word of God. Strength, power, deliverance, victory, and blessing come to those who wait.

Our waiting, however, involves our obedient action and response to His leading. There is a huge difference between delay or procrastination and waiting. If we are dragging our feet instead of moving in His leading and timing, that can be disobedience or rebellion. When God calls, let us readily and quickly obey—no more delay. No more dragging our feet. Let us get to work with our Father!

---

You can never cross the ocean until you have the courage to lose sight of the shore.
~ Christopher Columbus

# Revival is Here

But you shall receive power
when the Holy Spirit comes upon you...
~ Acts 1:8

**Revival is not an event we are waiting for.** As we spend more time in the fellowship of the table, His table, we come to understand that our definition, explanation, and expectation of revival must change. Revival is not relegated to the future. *We who were once dead have now been made alive in Christ Jesus!* So, revival is not optional. We are not dead! We are renewed. We are alive! We must not slack off or let up. We must fully live. Revival is here and available now—**you are revival!**

Why revival? Why is it important to have a proper understanding of revival? We must be aware of the necessity of a long-term continuous move of God. His power is always available, and He is always moving among His people. It is our responsibility to become increasingly aware of His Presence, and we must focus on the importance of His Word and His Presence in our life at all times. This must be our utmost priority. It is too easy to become distracted and yield to pressures and compromises from the dark world around us. We must press in to persevere, trusting in our Lord. It is time to turn to Him! Acknowledge Him and receive!

There is only one hope for our land. There is only one thing that will save our nations. There is only one thing that will change any and all current situations, and that one thing is the Lord Jesus Christ! Jesus is the answer! Nothing else will save us. There is no deliverance, hope, power, or alternative. In her book, *First of All... and the Awakenings,* Billye Brim recalled a word from the Lord from 2008, "One thing will save America... and that is an awakening to God. One thing will avail for Israel and the nations. It is an awakening to God"[40] This is absolutely true.

What is a revival? What is an awakening? What is the difference between an awakening and a revival? Many thoughts, traditions, observations, and opinions exist on this subject. However, the two are very similar. Generally, revival is a locally contained outpouring of the Spirit of God. At the same time, an awakening is a more widespread or national movement where people begin to realize their need for the Presence and Power of God. The following quote from Patrick Morley sums it up very nicely: ***Revival and awakening are, generally, synonyms. The larger the geography a revival covers, the greater the tendency to call it an awakening. America has a deep, rich history of revivals and awakenings.*** [41]

Thank God we have this history of awakenings and revival. We must continue to desire, believe and return to that. Some definitions of revival are: "an act or instance of reviving; the state of being revived; renewed attention or interest in something; restoration of force, validity or effect."[42] Awakening is defined as: "a rousing from sleep; a rousing from inactivity or indifference; a revival of interest in something; a coming into awareness."[43] The Bible speaks of the importance of and our need for revival. Let us be awakened from our sleep and our complacency. Be revived! Step into the River of God. Let the outpouring of His Spirit fall on us. We must be revived. We must be awakened. The Spirit of God is being poured out upon His people! His Presence is available for us.

> Do this, knowing that this is a critical time. It is already the hour for you to awaken from your sleep [of spiritual complacency]; for our salvation is nearer to us now than when we first believed [in Christ]. (Romans 13:11 AMP)

> And that, knowing the time, that now it is high time to awake out of sleep: for now is our salvation nearer than when we believed. (Romans 13:11 KJV)

> Furthermore, knowing the time, now is the moment to awake from sleep. For now our salvation is nearer than when we believed. (Romans 13:11)

> Will You not revive us again, that Your people may rejoice in You? (Psalm 85:6)

For I will pour water on him who is thirsty, and floods on the dry ground; I will pour out My Spirit on your descendants, and My blessing on your offspring. (Isaiah 44:3)

On the last and greatest day of the feast, Jesus stood and cried out, "If anyone is thirsty, let him come to Me and drink. He who believes in Me, as the Scripture has said, out of his heart shall flow rivers of living water." By this He spoke of the Spirit, whom those who believe in Him would receive. (John 7:37-39)

He who is coming after me is mightier than I, whose shoes I am not worthy to carry. He will baptize you with the Holy Spirit and with fire. (Matthew 3:11)

"In the last days it shall be," says God, "that I will pour out My Spirit on all flesh;" (Acts 1:17)

And look, I am sending the promise of My Father upon you. But wait in the city of Jerusalem until you are clothed with power from on high. (Luke 24:49)

How hungry are we for the things of God? Are we willing to forsake all else and run to Him? Will you jump completely into His River? A great definition and description of revival came from the pastor of Northview Church in Columbus, Indiana. This statement is from a leader who has completely immersed himself, his family, and his church in a constant outpouring of the Spirit of God. In his book *River Rising,* Pastor Randall Burton states, "I'm not after revival, at least not as some understand and desire revival. I'm after a deeper and more personal relationship with God, the Holy Ghost."[44]

There is no better cure and solution for every problem in our nation and in our churches than to seek after this type of relationship. Our God is ready to grant us this precious and intimate fellowship with Him. It is time for us to awaken to the Presence of God! It is time to allow the Holy Spirit to revive us again!

A revival is not just an annual *special* meeting. Revival is so much more than just a series of meetings or conferences. Revival is our chance to get "face-to-face, heart-to-heart, and knee-to-knee"[45] with the Lord. A revival, awakening, refreshing, renewal, outpouring, or movement cannot be contained to one individual, one place, or one period. **Our expectations must rise.** Our anticipation must increase. God has not called us to *the Table* merely for a social gathering or religious affair. We have been called into His Presence to feast at **His Table** and enjoy His Presence. Revival is at *the Table!*

A God of fire is the only one there is.
Our God is not like an iceberg but like a forest fire.
He is never compared to the moon with its cool glow
but rather to the sun, radiating warmth.
He dwells in the light of the rising sun.
Whatever he does shines brightly and is carried out
with burning desire and a blazing purpose.
~ Reinhard Bonnke

# You're Equipped for Service

# Be Filled

Blessed are those who hunger and thirst for
righteousness, for they shall be filled.
~ Matthew 5:6

**There has never been a better time** to take full advantage of the opportunities and blessings that our Great God has freely provided for us. It is time to step into the full service of God. His Table is ready. The time is right. Reports of great moves of God are flooding in from all over the United States. The Holy Spirit has been moving mightily among all peoples. A fresh wave of His power and glory has swept through our colleges and universities. Praise God! It is a precious sight to see college students touched and overwhelmed by the power of God. What a tremendous blessing to see children enthralled and captivated by the great Presence of our Almighty God!

What about you? Where are you right now? Have you fully allowed God to have complete control over your heart and your life? Have you completely surrendered to Him? If not, this is the perfect opportunity to do so. It is no accident that you have received this material at this time. It is no coincidence that you are reading this chapter at this very moment. Repent and return to God right now. Submit and surrender to Him. Give Him every part of your life. **You can trust Him.** He will not let you down. He is more than able to see you through every situation and circumstance in your life.

I can remember so vividly sitting in church with my grandmother. She was one of the most awesome ladies I have ever known. There was no one like her. She was a member of the Church of God (with headquarters in Cleveland, TN), and I loved to go to church with her. Her church was exciting. At that time, the small church met on 14th Street in Paragould, Arkansas. I did not understand it then, but I later learned that what was so special about church with Grandma had little to do with her (even though it was a precious and rare opportunity to be there with her).

It had nothing to do with the music—although it was powerful, energetic, and loud, which was completely opposite of the style at my home church. It even had little to do with the excitement and shouts of the people. It had everything to do with the Presence of God. God was in that place. His precious Holy Spirit was there.

As I grew older, I longed for what I experienced there. It was… ***His Presence.*** I wanted so badly to let go of all the religious bondage and baggage that held me back. Still, I did not understand how to step out in faith and fully trust Him. It was not until many years later, as a young adult, that God spoke to me and gave me the directive and the correction needed to step out in obedient faith and respond to His leading and His prompting.

It is a tragic tendency and regular response of religion to strip away the intimacy of our relationship with our Lord. Still,

70

the truth is that God wants (and always has desired) a relationship with us. God has called us to devoted fellowship. He invites us into a close and personal walk with Him. No one knows us as God does. No one loves us as He does. We cannot trust anyone as we can trust Him. People fail. People fall. God will never fail. He will never leave us, forsake us, or abandon us.

We have a Divine invitation to fellowship. God has given us a special opportunity to receive greatly. We are blessed to visit and communicate with Him. Our relationship with Jesus is real, vital, and personal. He is our Lord. He is our Savior. He has provided beautiful and precious access to the Presence of the Father. Time spent with Him is not just a ritualistic or ceremonial religious encounter. It is a precious, intimate, glorious time of refreshing renewal and strength. Think about this: we are seated with Christ![46] We have a seat at *the Table*... **His Table.**

It is time to enjoy this fellowship and walk with God. It is time to allow His Spirit to engulf every aspect of our life. It is time to be filled to overflowing capacity with His Holy Spirit. We must stop holding back and limiting the flow of His Presence and power in our life. As mentioned, but worthy of repeating, God is pouring out His Spirit greatly in our colleges and universities. He is pouring out His Spirit upon ALL flesh.[47] Holy Spirit is moving on ALL people. He is doing mighty and great works. I want to be smack dab in the middle of it! I do not want to miss this move of God, and I do not want you to miss this move.

We had the great joy of experiencing a mighty move of God that began in the late fall of 2012. We had just relocated to pastor a church in Dyersburg, Tennessee. Evangelist Charles Walters was scheduled to minister with us for a three-day meeting. God moved mightily in those weekend services, so much so that what was originally scheduled as a one-weekend event unfolded into a five-week encounter!

In the light of many other great moves of God, this may seem insignificant; however, these meetings developed in our hearts a true desire and passion for a move of God like never before. In the years following this outpouring, God continued to stir our hearts and increase our faith. In 2016, God took us to a new level in Him, and we saw many great things begin in our ministry. The Presence and power of God were so rich and powerful during those meetings. There was a moving of His Presence and glory that was intense and invigorating. There were salvations, deliverances, re-dedications, healings, and powerful times of simply sitting in the beautiful heavy Presence of God.

The training and developing time in His Presence is so powerful. He taught us so much during this season. Reflecting on these years, I am reminded of the many answered prayers and the great peace in that church. God brought many things into fulfillment and manifestation during this time.

For example, God began to prepare our hearts for that very moment fourteen years *before* this season of outpouring. Pastor Luis Torres, an evangelist at the time, visited our church in Albuquerque, New Mexico. I was a young worship leader, just beginning in the ministry. Pastor Torres prayed and prophesied over me during one of those nights. He asked God to anoint me to lead the church in worship. Further, he spoke that God would anoint me to write songs about revival and the Presence of God.

We have seen this prayer come to pass. It is important to note that most of the original songs God gave me are about those very things. Many of those songs were composed during the revival meetings of that season. What a joy that God gave these songs, gifts for His glory and His people.

Many years later as Evangelist Linda Brewer spoke into my life about this very book, God gave her an inside look into our ministry, much like He had done with Pastor Torres. With detail, she spoke about the things God had given me and how they were put in a set place and in specific files. She reminded me that they were given to me for God to use!

These are a few examples, witnesses that *revival is here!* It has never left. Thank God, the Presence of our Lord has been here since the creation of His Church on the Day of Pentecost. He is pouring out His Spirit today and granting good gifts to His children. Father God ministers daily to His Church. He wants to bless us more than we could ever imagine. He so wants us to be aware of His Presence and anointing.

It is our responsibility to continue in the things of God. We are to develop the desire and longing for His Presence. God wants us to live in the moves of His Spirit every day and every moment. In Acts 2:17 and Joel 2:28, God promised to pour out of His Spirit on ALL flesh. All means ALL. Everyone on the face of the earth – young and old; men and women; all classes of people, and all nations are included.

Further, Peter summed it up in Acts 2:39 as he explained that this very promise is for "you and your children and to ALL who are afar off, even as many as the Lord our God shall call."[48] We can experience the fullness of the Holy Spirit. We can be filled with the Spirit. Paul taught this powerful truth in Ephesians 5:18. He instructed the Ephesian believers to "Be filled with the Spirit." This is an ongoing action and a dedicated, determined choice. Choose to be *continuously* filled with the Holy Spirit! We must always remain filled with the Holy Spirit. We must remain under His influence and filled to the max with His precious Holy Spirit! A decision, determination, and a desire for a never-ending moving, filling, and equipping of the Spirit.

---

Lord, I pray for a never-ending move of God.
Let the fire and fresh anointing abide in me,
Flowing out to the hearts of the hopeless
and the lost in need.
I pray for a never-ending move of God.[49]
~ Rita King-Chadwick

# A Whole New Level
# of God's Anointing

The Spirit of the Lord is upon Me because
He has anointed Me to preach the gospel
to the poor; He has sent Me to heal the
broken-hearted, to preach deliverance to the
captives and recovery of sight to the blind,
to set at liberty those who are oppressed;
preach the acceptable year of the Lord.
~ Luke 4:18-19

**We are anointed for the service of the Lord.** God's anointing is so precious, and He has placed His seal of approval upon us. As God's anointing comes upon us, there is an overwhelming abundance of the power of God available to do the work He has called us to do. His anointing equips the believer and makes all the difference in our lives and ministry. As Jesus instructed His believers at His ascension, we must be endued with power from on high.[50] Jesus was anointed to preach, heal, save, and deliver.[51] He has authorized, commissioned, and anointed us to do the same. It is time to step into a higher level of His anointing and power.

We are in Christ. His anointing is upon us. He has given us the authority to step into the same available power in Him. Jesus taught us that as His believers and followers of Him, *great-*

75

*er works* would be done in our life and ministry.[52] It is time for us to accept the mantle and assignment given to us, and we must do so with His anointing.

In these last days, the child of God should see miracles, signs, and wonders every day. According to the final instructions of our Lord Jesus, such signs follow the believer. It is the time to be bold-believing believers. This is the season for the miraculous. We are in the territory of the supernatural working and manifestation of the power and demonstration of our God! God has called His people to a ministry of great power and anointing. It is His desire for His people to be free. He desires for His children to be healed. He wants us to have true sight. This is the truth of the gospel. Jesus saves. Jesus heals. Jesus delivers. Jesus sets every captive free.

> You prepare a table before me in the presence
> of my enemies, You anoint my head with oil;
> My cup runs over. (Psalm 23:5)

> You have anointed me with fresh oil. (Psalm
> 92:10)

Not only has our great God prepared a table and a place at *the Table,* but He has anointed our head with fresh oil in the presence of our enemies. He has placed His divine power, authority, and ability upon us.

Break free with the breakthrough anointed power of God. He has provided so much for us. Why would we not want to step into the fullness of His amazing power, strength, and ability? Living and walking in the Spirit-empowered anointed life is much better. There is great power in the anointing. There is great protection in the anointing. There is precious healing in His anointing. True stability rests in His anointing. This anointing preserves and propels the people of God to properly perform His work and duty.

When we limit the anointing to only what is pleasing to us, we have completely missed the importance and significance thereof. Too many well-meaning individuals have confused or mistaken the anointing of God for fleshly manifestations, talents, gifts, or responses. Someone is not anointed because they sing or preach well. Singers and preachers should be anointed. However, our reception and appreciation of the singer, song, preacher, or sermon do not indicate such anointing. It is not anointed simply because we enjoy it or because of a certain response from the crowd. The anointing is the manifested power of God in an individual's life for service and ministry. It has little to do with our response, feeling, or preference.

There will always be a response to the anointing. God's power at work will change things. We must be willing to receive from Him and His Word.

What God has anointed is of tremendous value. God has anointed His Word. It is saturated with all the ingredients of the anointing of God—every passage, every book, every verse is full of power, anointing, and authority. God has anointed His people. We must recognize the power of God working in our lives. We must submit to the power of God in our lives. Brothers and sisters, let the anointing flow. Let the power of

God manifest in your situation. Let Him fill you to overflowing today.

Every believer should see the regular manifestation of the power of God every day of their life. Each new day is a brand-new opportunity to experience more of the power and Presence of God. Every morning, the mercies of the Lord are new and fresh.[53] He has a fresh anointing and assignment for His people every day. Fresh revelation, strength, and power are available every step of the way as we follow Jesus.

Our great God has blessed us in the past. However, this is His day. This is His season. He has something new, fresh, significant, and relevant right now. Blessings and treasures are ready for us every time we submit and turn to Him. He desires to pour out more upon you than you could ever imagine. This is the perfect time to lift your hands to Him and begin to receive a fresh anointing! Let Him refresh you with His precious Holy Spirit. Right now, thank Him for His many magnificent blessings. Thank Him for His great and overflowing mercy and goodness in your life. Praise Him for this season of your life and ministry. Watch as He begins to move and operate as you give Him the space and time to do so. Go ahead. Let Him take you to a new level of His anointing and power. Enjoy this place of ministry. Enjoy this time of refilling! Enjoy this season of blessing, honor, and glory in His Presence! Bow before Him and worship at His Table!

Why would we ever want to hold back? Why would we ever want to limit His ability in our life? Recently, our friend Evangelist Charles Walters was ministering at our church in Texas.

It was an extraordinary weekend of God's glory and power. Before the scheduled services, God had given a young man in our church the desire to make some anointing oil. Some of this oil was prepared and bottled up as gifts for the Evangelist and other special guests. The remaining oil was placed in a large pitcher of clay. During the first night of the meeting, Brother Charles dipped a handkerchief into this anointing oil. He used it as he ministered and prayed over various service participants.

After the conclusion of the service, I made sure everything was put away and ready for the next scheduled meeting. I noticed the pitcher and placed the handkerchief on the top of this earthen vessel. As we arrived for the service the next evening, I walked by this pitcher and noticed the handkerchief. I watched as the anointing oil dripped off the handkerchief onto other handkerchiefs below.

Immediately the Lord began to speak to me, and He said, **"Be the handkerchief."** "Be the handkerchief." What on earth does this mean? The Lord repeated it, and as He repeated it, I noticed as the oil dripped again. As I looked at the other clothes under the pitcher, I noticed how saturated they had become. The once dry and isolated hanky had now become a vessel of anointing, transferring such a level of rich anointing into everything else. It had been completely immersed and saturated with the things of God and now was, in turn, saturating those around it. God has a whole new level of His anointing available to us. Let us receive ALL HE has for us!

---

With everything you are facing right now, know
that you have an anointing to face, overcome,
restore, transform, and see change come to it. Why?
Because the Spirit of the Lord God is upon you! He
has anointed you! You are anointed for this!

~ Judy Jacobs

# Enjoy and Celebrate

Rejoice in the Lord always.
Again I will say, rejoice!
~ Phillppians 4:4

**God has anointed us.** Hallelujah! It is celebration time. He has called us and has prepared a place for us. He has prepared a great place for us. God has given us the most precious opportunity, and it is unfolding more and more each day before us. His Spirit is constantly at work among us. He has given so much to us, His children. What a tremendous privilege to enjoy the many great blessings and benefits freely given to us through our Lord Jesus Christ! It is time to enjoy!

There is no guilt or shame in thoroughly enjoying your walk and relationship with the Lord. Accept His invitation and partake of every blessing and benefit He has provided you. Fill yourself with the great things readily and freely available in Christ.

Why would anyone hold back any longer? Jump right into the fullness of God. Enjoy every moment. Take it ALL! We do not have to pick and choose. Jesus has made everything available right now! It is done. It is forever settled. It is finished. He left nothing and no one out. Walk in the power, authority, and unction that is before you.

Enjoy! Rejoice! Christians should be the most joyful, pleasant people in the world. The Word of God we have received and our fellowship with Him brings us great joy. An indescribable joy—a joy that is beyond understanding. There is no other way to live.

Joy is a choice. Choose to be glad. This is the day I will be glad. The Lord has made this day. He has made me glad! Today is the day. His victory is mine. I am blessed, anointed, chosen, and highly favored by the Lord.

Choose joy again. Choose to take strength in ALL God has provided. True joy is never based on circumstances or situations. True joy is fully trusting Jesus as Lord. This joy and trust are found when we completely rest in Him and His finished work. It is such a joy to know and serve Him. He is always bringing great things to us. His peace, provision, protection, power, and promise are always available at work.

I choose Him again! I choose Him today; therefore, I rejoice. Therefore, I am glad. He is my complete strength, hope, and confidence. Praise God, I believe Him, and I know He is my Rewarder and my great reward![54] I completely trust Him. I rest in Him. He is my God, and I will praise Him!

Remember, the joy of the Lord is your strength![55] When we choose His joy, we choose His strength. When we stand in His joy, we are covered and anointed with His power, strength, and might.

There is no loss, lack, or lag in the joy of the Lord. Other words to describe the joy that is available to us in the Lord are celebrate, delight, enjoy, glory, and triumph.[56] We should have a glorious triumphant, delightful celebration of His joy every day!

God has so much for us. He has provided so many wonderful things for us. God has blessed us so richly. He has given above and beyond what we could ever expect or dream. Open your eyes. Lift your head. Stand firm. Rise. Know who you are and to Whom you belong. Enjoy what He has at *the Table* for you.

God's good provision is for you.

He knows how to take good care of you.

He knows what is best.

He has the best ways to get His great blessing, gifts, and benefits to you!

Trust Him. Follow His plan. Accept His invitation.
**Come to the Table… take your seat!**

---

Faith expects from God
what is beyond all expectation.
~ Andrew Murray

# Appendix

# Notes

1   John 10:10
2   Ephesians 3:20
3   John 2:5
4   Merriam-webster.Com dictionary, s.V. "Inspiration," accessed July 27, 2022, https://www.Merriam-webster.Com/dictionary/inspiration.
5   2 Peter 1:2-4
6   Genesis 1:28
7   Luke 2:49
8   John 14:6; Ephesians 2:18
9   Philippians 4:13
10  2 Corinthians 10:12
11  2 Corinthians 5:21; 1 Corinthians 1:30
12  Mark 16:15;
13  John 3:16
14  Ephesians 4:11-16
15  Matthew 6:33
16  James 2:17
17  Matthew 19:26; Mark 9:23; Mark 10:27; Luke 18:27
18  Habakkuk 2:2
19  Matthew 24:35; Mark 13:31; Luke 21:33
20  2 Timothy 4:2
21  Romans 10:15 NLT
22  James Strong, Strong's Expanded Exhaustive Concordance of the Bible (Nashville: Thomas Nelson, 2009), s.v. "beautiful."
23  Matthew 22:9-10; Luke 14:23

24 Matthew 16:18

25 Luke 17:26; Matthew 24:37

26 Genesis 6:8 NLT

27 John 14:6

28 Philippians 4:13

29 Isaiah 6:8

30 Hebrews 13:8

31 Sally Bruton Vann; "The Table;" *African Moons (Blog);* June 12, 2012; https://africanmoons.org/blog/the-table/

32 Jeremiah 29:11

33 2 Chronicles 16:9

34 Psalm 46

35 Philippians 4:19

36 Psalm 68:19

37 Hebrews 10:36

38 James Strong, Strong's Expanded Exhaustive Concordance of the Bible (Nashville: Thomas Nelson, 2009), s.v. "patience."

39 John 16:13

40 Billye Brim, *First of All & the Awakenings* (Branson: Billye Brim Ministries, 2017), 8.

41 Patrick Morley. "A Brief History of Spiritual Revival and Awakening in America." Church Leaders. October 12, 2022. A Brief History of Spiritual Revival and Awakening in America (churchleaders.com)

42 Merriam-Webster.com Dictionary, s.v. "revival," accessed March 3, 2023, https://www.merriam-webster.com/dictionary/revival.

43 Merriam-Webster.com Dictionary, s.v. "awakening," accessed March 3, 2023, https://www.merriam-webster.com/dictionary/awakening.

44 Randall E. Burton, *River Rising* (Mobile: Evergreen Press, 2015), 5-6.

45 Steve Youngblood

46 Ephesians 2:6

47 Acts 2:17

48 Acts 2:39 KJV

49 Rita King. "Never Ending Move of God." *Never Ending Move of God: Songs of Visitation.* Luis Torres Ministries, 1998, Cassette.

50 Luke 24:49

51 Luke 4:18-19

52 John 14:12

53 Lamentations 3:23

54 Hebrews 11:6

55 Nehemiah 8:10

56 Thesaurus.com Thesaurus, s.v. "rejoice" accessed March 15, 2023, https://www.thesaurus.com/browse/rejoice

# Meet the Author

Jason Houston is an anointed minister, teacher, and musician originally from Paragould, Arkansas. Pastor Houston is ordained with the Assemblies of God. He has a Bachelor of

 Music in Keyboard Performance from Arkansas State University. He ministers with boldness and love, following the leading of the Holy Spirit. He and his wife, Rachel, have pastored for over twenty years, serving in Missouri, Arkansas, New Mexico, Tennessee, and (currently) Texas. They have served the church in various capacities, from Music and Worship Pastors to Associate and Lead Pastors and Itinerant Ministers.

Before the ministry, Pastor Jason performed as a professional musician, working with artists such as Andy Williams, Pat Boone, Debby Boone, Glen Campbell, Robert Goulet, and many others. He is also a former Music Educator, teaching privately and publicly throughout his tenure in ministry. The Houston's reside in Clarendon, Texas, where they serve as Pastor of Clarendon First Assembly of God.

The Houston's are also the founders of Houston Faith Ministries, and they are the hosts of the daily WORD4Life broadcast, a live teaching and ministry broadcast streaming on multiple social media platforms.

This book is available at all major online booksellers or directly from the author.

To invite Pastor Jason Houston
to speak or to purchase additional copies,
please visit:

http://www.houstonfaithministries.com